Who Am I?

A collection of poetry captured in Oneness.

Inspired by my hearts willingness to stay open with the intention to illuminate love in all directions.

Prologue

I'm pretty sure the flow of this book came into reality floating down the green river in Utah with one of my dearest friends and teachers, Leslieann Hobayan. As if by osmosis her creative genius and skills as a poet enveloped me that week. We had never met each other before but somehow, we'd known each other for lifetimes. Without our connection this would not have happened.

Never in a million years did I imagine writing a book of poetry… this body of work moved through me. It has been a process of deep discovery, reflection, healing and realisation. It is not mine, nor do I feel it belongs to me.
It is ours.

It is my deepest wish to develop enlightened sensitivity for the benefit of all beings.
This book is an expression of that wish.
I am forever grateful for the opportunity to open and flourish in the work of the divine.

If no one ever reads this book,
I wouldn't care a damn.
What matters most
To me you see,
Is simply that…
I Am.

Gratitude

To my children, Troy and Taylor, who unlocked my heart so poetry could emerge… without the two of you none of this would have meaning.

To my husband, Lyle, who holds my heart so safe… because of you love is my anchor.

To my parents, Jeff and Carol, who gave me life and showed me the way, without you I could not have taken this direction.

To my sister, Candice, whose presence in my life has given me wholeness.

To the friends who co-created with me on these insights, epiphanies and writings, Natalie Propa and Candice Goldring, your support, encouragement, and belief in me brought this book to life.

Leopardo Yawa Bane whose wisdom and work is transforming the world - I am eternally grateful to your lineage and the blessings they have bestowed upon me.

Byron McClean whose strength and sacrifice in service facilitates impact immeasurable, because of you these words are wands.

Gail Harris, whose love of poetry sparked the flame that lit the path for this experience, your leadership continues to light flames of the future.

Breanna Pastor, your feedback, and encouragement positioned this book in my heart as something important to be shared. You are a shining star, and you light up the darkness.

To all the people, plants, animals, technology, and experiences that have touched my life… without everyone and everything… this would not be real.

I Am so grateful.

"The Question "Who Am I" is not really meant to get an answer,

the question "Who Am I?" is meant to dissolve the questioner."

Ramana Maharashi

NOW

What Time is it?

What time is it?
Do you know?
What time is it?
I think I'll grow.

Whatever it's time for
I Am here.
I'll make the most of now,
I'll make it clear.

Whenever it's time for something new,
There's a chance to see a different view.

What is it time for?
I'm excited…
Whatever it's time for,
I've been invited.

//The Invitation

Let this be my Guide

In the absence of proof
There is a need to believe,
Let this by my guide…
As I learn to concede.

As I discover the riches,
Of being here now.
I trust that this moment…
Teaches me how to bow.

The greater unknown
Always has its own plan.
When I slip into doubt…
I learn how to stand.

If I lean into grace,
And surrender to One.
In the void of the darkness…
Turn my face to the sun.

// In Faith

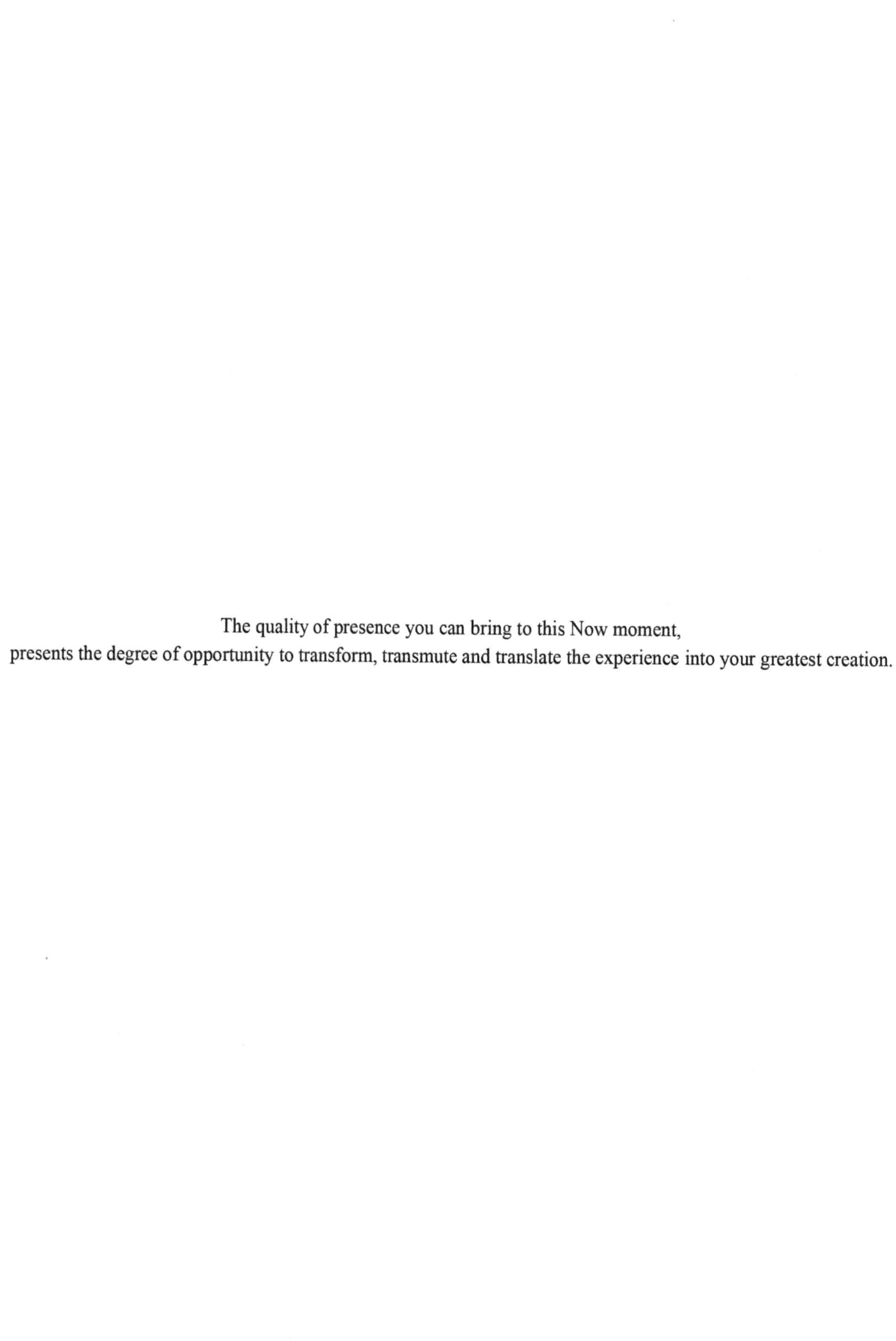

The quality of presence you can bring to this Now moment,
presents the degree of opportunity to transform, transmute and translate the experience into your greatest creation.

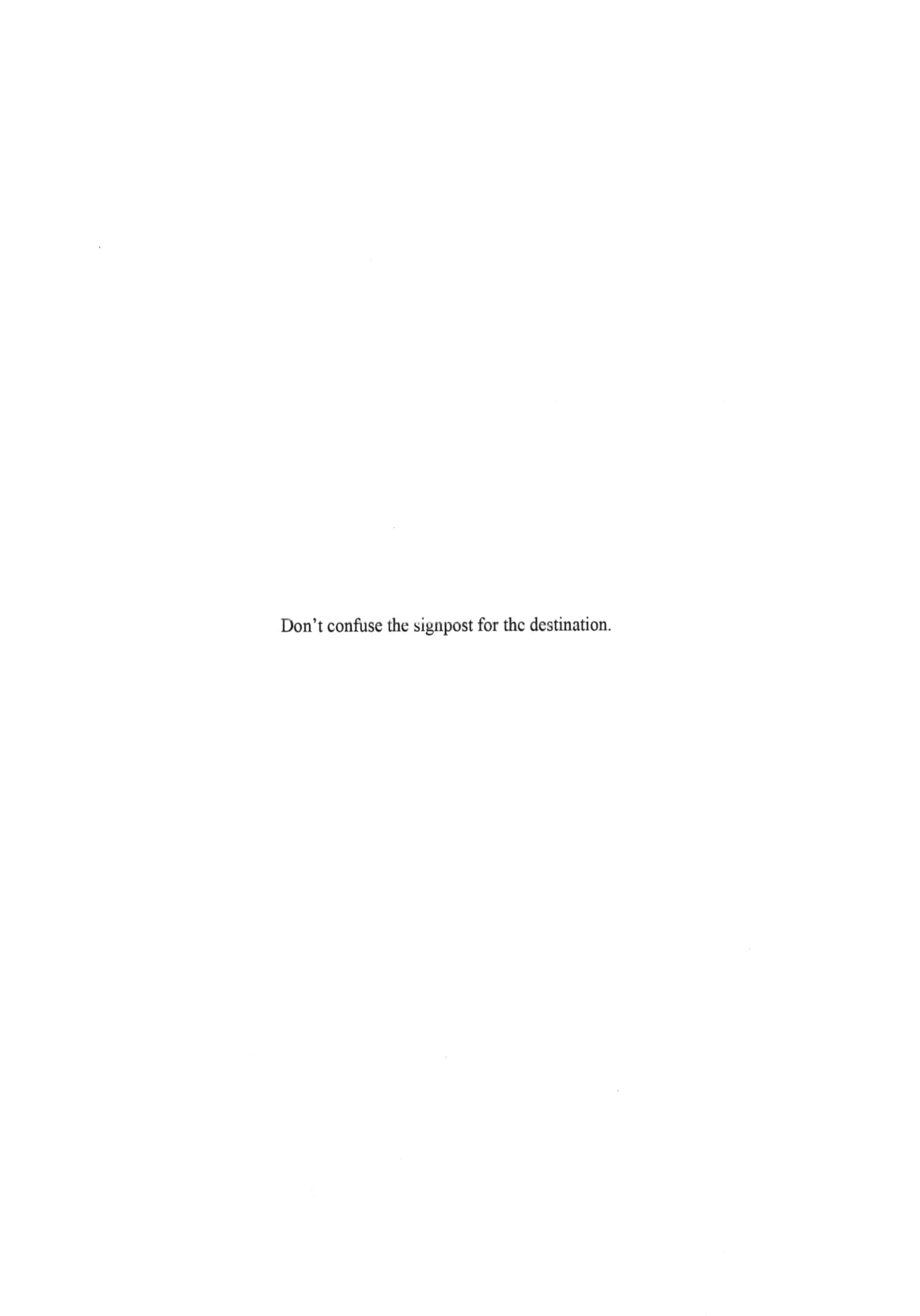

Don't confuse the signpost for the destination.

Every Season, A Reason

I trust there is a reason,
For every time
And every season…
Even though
I may not know
The meaning
At first…

But I trust there is a reason,
For every time
And every season…
And that meaning
Will eventually
Emerge.

For when I look back
On confusion,
What I find
Is the illusion,
That I know
What I need,
More so
Than God.

And when the Air begins to clear,
And I can finally start to hear…
What I learn is,
I believed
A facade.

For no One
Knows things better,
Than the eye
Of the creator.
And the truth
Is a powerful
Liberator.

And when I rest
In surrender
And I open up
To splendor
Everything
I ever needed
Is Now.

Equanimity

In the wide-open spaces
Of an empty mind,
Is a pathway to peace,
You're sure to find.

Letting go of the noise,
Taking in what's in sight,
A stillness of heart
A passage of rites.

Taking only essentials
I learn what I need,
The love of a family
Each one of us lead.

Take a deep breath
Move beyond memory
Walk through the void,
Equanimity.

We are all repeating patterns of the past, until they become conscious.
From there we can either change or choose to transform it into purpose.

Intention doesn't get the work done.
Action does.
Until then it's just keeping busy…
Find purpose.

Yours to Create

Every day, I learn, I grow.
I can do hard things,
This I know.

Every day, space opens up.
I choose the things,
That fill my cup.

Every day, new light appears.
A brand-new start,
Love's souvenirs.

Every day, A portal opens.
To create new worlds,
The wise have spoken.

What do you wish upon this day?
Whose life will you touch?
What will you say?

Whatever you do,
Make sure it's great.
Whatever you choose,
It's yours to create.

// The Choice

Anything Can Happen

What happened,
The last time you were open?

What happened,
The last time you went deep?

What happened,
The last time you felt vulnerable?

Did it wake you from your sleep?

What happened,
The last time you said "Yes!" to life?

The last time
You chose to change?

Was it good for you?
Did you feel alive?
Did you want to try again?

Where did you go?
Do you know?
Who did you meet there, then?

What happens next?
Will you grow?
Will you say "Yes!" again, and when?

What do you need?
What do you wish?
What is your biggest passion?

Each time we open,
Potential shows us,
Anything can happen…

//In Neutrality

There is wisdom in staying open AND saying no to things that don't move in the direction of our dreams…

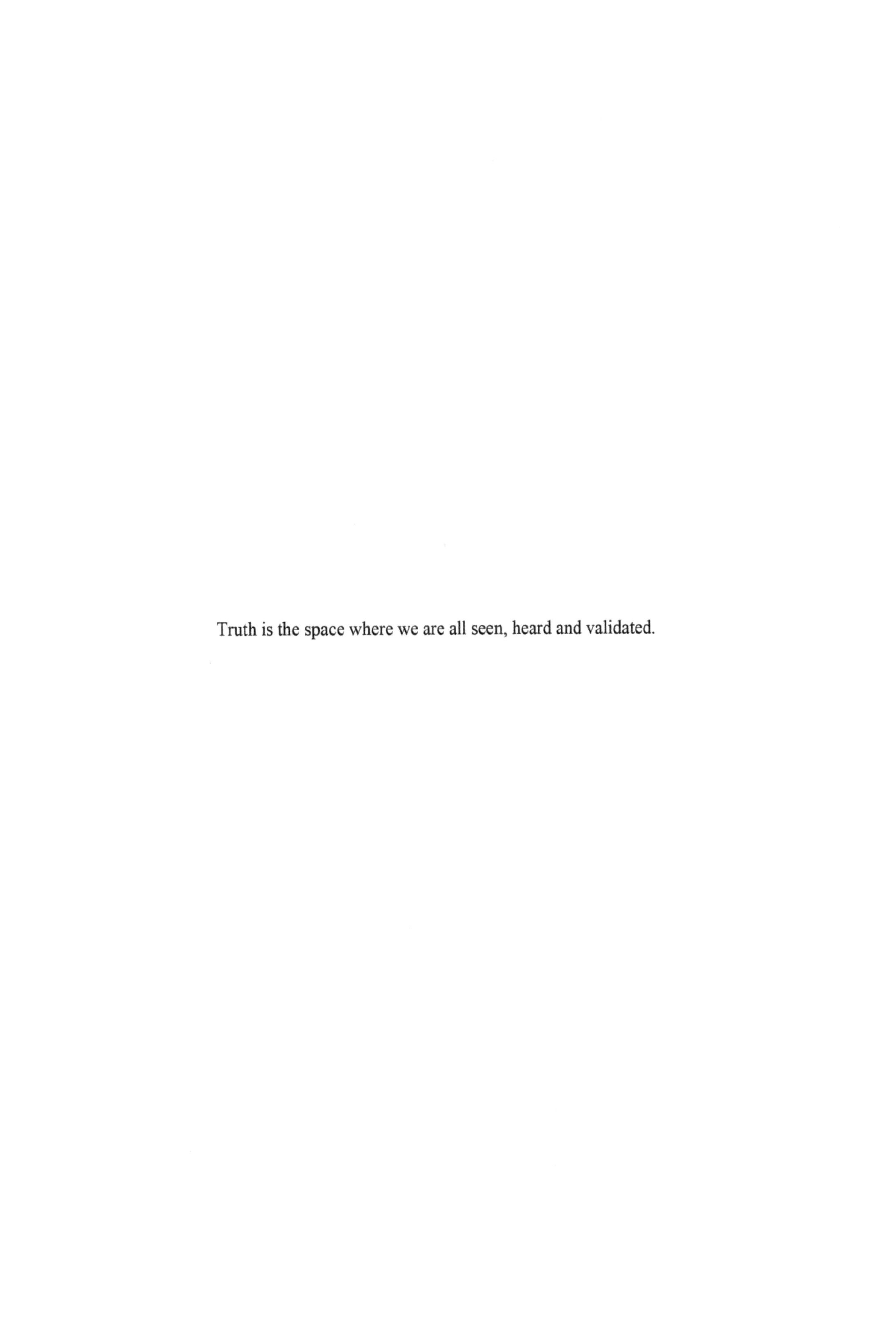

Truth is the space where we are all seen, heard and validated.

Feel your Heart

There is a time for this…
And time for that.
Time to move,
And then step back.

There is time to wonder,
And then sit still.
Time to focus,
And then explore.

There is time to rest,
And time to serve.
There is time for action,
And just observe.

There is time to speed up,
And then slow down.
There is time for love
And then there's none…

There may be more time,
There may be not.
There's only now
To feel your heart.

//A Time for it All

Into the Sacred

I call it into sacred,
This moment I Am in.
No matter where I find myself,
I know there's love within.

I surrender into sacred,
The experience,
Here,
Now.
Because I know what's moving through me,
Is bigger than me somehow.

I release into the sacred,
Trusting to the bone.
It's not always very comfortable,
Feeling the expanse of the unknown.

I stand up in the sacred,
This is my chosen way.
I wish to see the light it shines,
Spirit has the final say.

//On The Journey

THE PATH

The Bridge

I Am the bridge.
And I'm pointing to a place,
Where we all can come together.
Where we all feel safe to say…

This is where I'm at,
I know there's work to do.
But I'll take it at my pace,
And I trust that you will too.

And while we're working
Back to Oneness,
Old beliefs come to confront us.
This is where we meet,
Let the heart become our compass.

//Feet in all the worlds

The Path of Potential

The path of potential…
Where does it go?
There is work to be done,
Dreams left to sew.

The path of potential…
Has unlimited routes.
We're each living one of them,
On the commute…

The path of potential…
Can only lead home.
To the place we remember,
In the unknown.

The path of potential…
Has so much to see.
There's nothing to fear,
-     Destiny.

//Exploring Potential

Re-Planted

It may be that it gets worse at first,
But don't get too attached.
"This too shall pass",
My mother said.
Her balanced view unmatched.

When things are hard,
It's okay to struggle…
I'm learning this is valid.
Soon enough it shifts
And from the depths,
A new dimension added.

For every time we go full circle,
The world's a little bigger.
We expand you see,
With every loop-
The hard stuff is the trigger.

So, when next you're feeling super low,
Remember this is grounding.
We need our roots,
To stay firmly planted,
So our branches can surround us.

Every tree comes from a seed,
We're never on our own.
If you look around,
You're sure to find,
The others who are home.

Re-planting in a bigger land
Can make us feel the smallest,
And when the sprouts push past the surface,
You See the wonder of the forest.

// In Transformation

Written in collaboration with my father, Jeff Lopes, someone I am honored to call a guide on my path.

Being held in a process
May feel like I'm stuck…
Like nothing is happening,
Being here, is the luck.

There's magic unfolding,
It's brewing with care…
Just slow down a minute,
Breathe in the air.

When the moment arrives
Something new will be birthed.
It's growing inside…
This must happen first.

So, whilst I am waiting
And can't see the growth,
I'll trust for a time,
It has to be both…

How many times has it broken your spirit?
And yet you get back up.
How many times have you lost your way?
And still, you get unstuck.
How many times have you been defeated?
Too many to count, I'd guess.
How many times have you wished it would end?
Yet you keep saying "Yes!"

The experience has infinite ways…
To show you your potential.
If you stay open and willing to change…
You'll remain experiential.

Collective Co-Creation

What moves through us when we're together?
This is how we share our treasure…

What parts of One show up in presence?
This is how I explore our essence.

How do we connect in this now moment?
We're both learning, two complete components.

What parts of me grow when I'm with you?
I am grateful for the work you do.

And as I observe the unfolding experience,
I wonder why we need to hear this?

Am I doing my best to be in spirit?
And then I trust, remembering All-That-Is.

Our evolution is a process of integration.
This is our collective co-creation.

// In Collaboration

A Shared Canoe with You

I see you there,
We've never met,
For some reason,
I want to greet you.

You say "Hello",
And then I know,
I am here,
Destined to meet you.

Your smiling eyes
Are full of light,
Your heart
Is shining brightly.

"Would you like to Share a canoe with me?"
-    "Sure."
You say Politely.

And as we float,
Beyond the great unknown
I discover you're a poet,
But not the kind that only rhymes,
The kind that deeply knows It…

// In Osmosis

In recognition of my beautiful friendship with Leslieann and how we continue to discover fuller Truths.
Her heart touched mine.

Beautiful Blind Spots

I have so many blind spots…
I cannot escape them.
So many blind spots…
Could I forsake them?

These patches of darkness,
Looking for light.
Seeking attention…
Wanting respite.

I have so many blind spots…
I'm ready to see.
These beautiful blind spots,
Teaching me
How to Be.

//The Beauty of Blind spots

Grieving Innocence

Where did you go to?
That place I called home…
Where did you go to?
I want to know.

In the stillness, I'm quiet.
As tears flood my cheeks…
How did I get here?
I feel so weak…

Why is this happening?
-        Surely it can't…
My dreams have dissolved.
Who served this grant?

It can only be me…
-     Wait where are the others?
We're in this together.
Call in the mothers!

What do you need?
What has to happen?
We are all held as One.
Just start to imagine…

There is a reason…
For all of the times.
You can't see it now,
Just sit tight and find…

It all has to happen,
And ensure that you do…
Practice the magic
That's right within you.

//Held

Finding Faith

Some may think that faith's
A soft skill…
A detachment from polarity.
Some blind surrender,
That just let's go…

But no.

This place clarity.

Some may think that faith
Is gentle…
An acceptance of
What's bazaar.

But no…

Faith stands up and faces
And points to the north star.

Some may think that faith
Is blissful…
A one sided
Solution.

But no.

Faith is depth of understanding.
The direction of evolution.

Some may think that faith
Is personal…
A lonely inner
Strength.

But no.

Faith says, "We're together."
Together we swim the length.

//In Faith

Travelling Light

Life will feel easier,
When you're travelling light.
Let go what's not needed,
To create what's in sight.

Hold on if you want to…
That's okay too.
I trust what you choose,
Is what's right for you.

Just know there's a choice,
It's for you to decide.
When you're ready to shift,
It comes from the inside.

When you can't see the choice,
Just listen some more…
This moment's our teacher
There are blessings -
Explore.

//Awareness

In times of great darkness,
It may be easy to find…
What's going wrong?
It's time to be kind.

Don't give up hope,
The end is in sight…
Keep looking inward,

I Am the light.

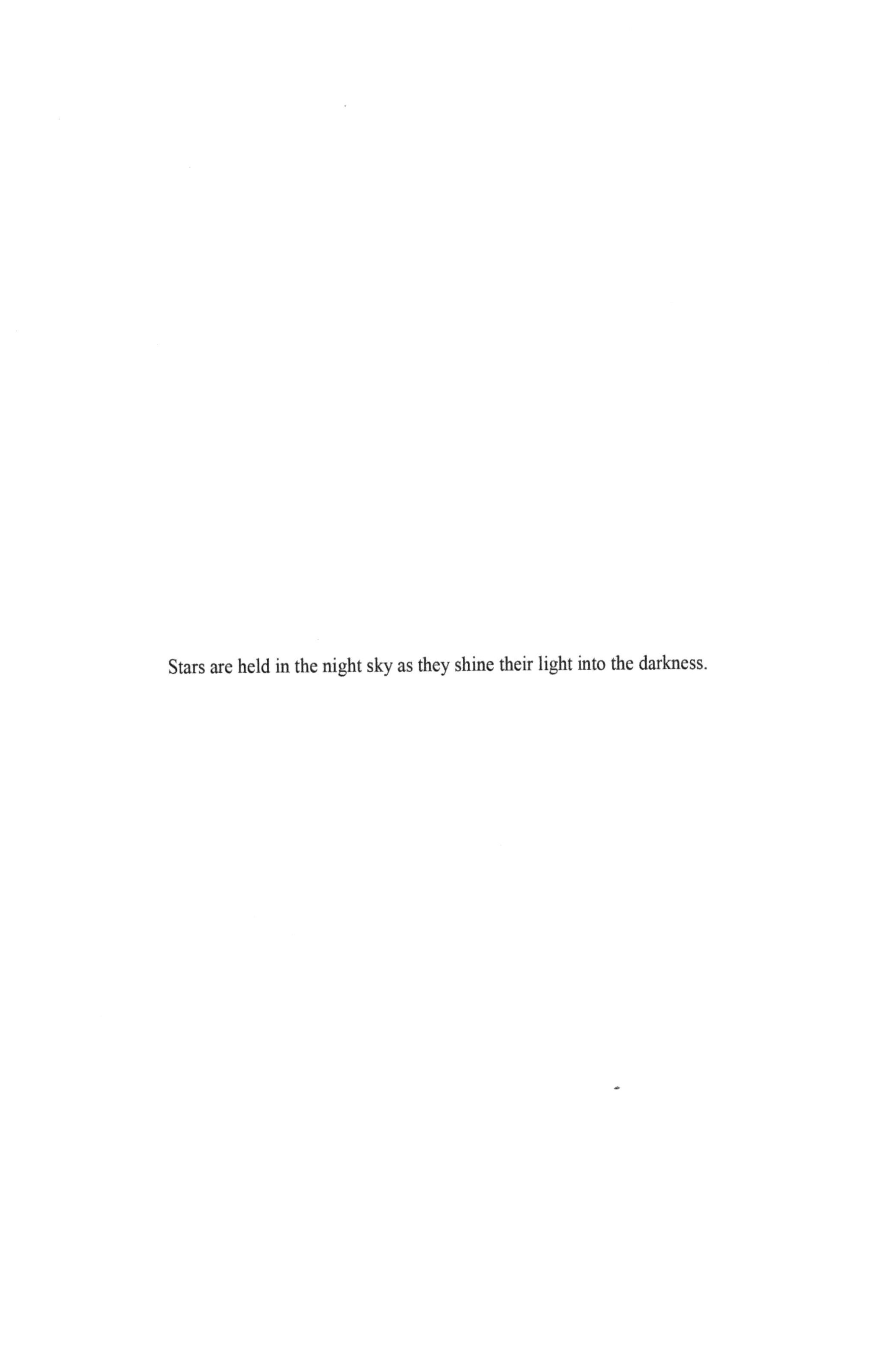

Stars are held in the night sky as they shine their light into the darkness.

Resume

It's hard to carry darkness,
It's hard to be the light.
It's hard to anchor love,
With so much suffering in sight.

It's hard to see the beauty,
When the mess
Is hard to clear,
It's hard to stand in purpose,
With the ground
Shifting in fear.

It's hard to come to stillness,
When my heart feels
Cold with fright.
It's hard to make peace
Here at home.

Is this eternal night?

The stars keep shining brightly,
Showing me the way.
When I Am quiet
In my knowing,
Spirit comes to say:

The spark is you beloved,
Go within and see
Everything's impermanent,
Your heart's always been free.
The change comes from inside you,
I Am here to watch you bloom,
When you're ready to commit to love,

The journey may resume.

//Transmutation

Beautiful Illusions

These beautiful illusions,
Evolve with me through time.
Have me questioning reality…
And wondering what's mine.

These beautiful illusions,
Continue to expand.
Creating more desires…
Where do I choose to stand?

These beautiful illusions,
Teach me how to be Love.
Cementing hope & freedom…
Through wise ones up above.

With the stars above to guide me,
I look up to them in awe.
As I honor them in wisdom,
Feet firmly on the floor.

Keep shining on, in order.
Light the path through the unknown.
As I find my way through space time,
Awareness seeds are sewn.

//Evolving Ignorance

In the Shadow of Awareness

In the shadow of awareness,
Something comes to change…
In the shadow of awareness,
We can begin to start again.

In the shadow of awareness,
We can become the light of One,
If we're brave enough to grow,
The transformation has begun.

It's only through the shadows,
That the light is found within,
Before then it may have seemed
It was outside the skin we're in.

But the darkness is a gift,
The unexamined parts of self.
The places deep inside us
We've forgotten hold great wealth.

What is the light without a shadow?
Would we even know the difference?
The experience of contrast comes to show us,
Our own ignorance.

We need not choose to visit darkness,
When we've found our light- we have the tools.
Darkness comes and we stand bravely,
To recover more of love's hidden jewels.

// Fruitful Darkness

More Aware

Guilty pleasures,
Sweet relief…
Why does it make
Me feel so weak?

Shame released,
Just agree…
All is valid,
Meet the need.

Once surrendered
All is well…
This too shall pass,
Judgement
Expelled.

No one harmed
I let go,
Evolution…
And so I grow.

I flow through this,
And find its whole.
There is beauty here,
It plays its role.

I'll ride the wave
From here to there…
I'll keep my heart,
It's more Aware.

//In Shame

The things I've earned,
Help me discern -
The experiences I want,
And what I deserve.

To reject/accept anything completely is to negate it's potential for wholeness.

And while we are free to explore in our own directions of interest,
to recognise wholeness means crossing paths with every being peacefully.

So that one day we may realise our Oneness.

Feel The Burn

When you're feeling the fire,
And have nowhere to turn.
Just sit for a minute…
Feel the burn.

It might feel like anger,
With rising heat.
But try to come inwards…
Pull up a seat.

Fire transforms us,
It's kills what was dead.
It needed to end…
"It is Time", my heart said.

The best thing to do,
When you want to leave,
Is to follow your heart…
Let your heart lead.

Where will it take me?
I don't really know…
What feels right?
I'm still learning to flow…

One thing's for sure,
My heart knows the way.
Just try to surrender
And stand up and Say:

I promise to feel, this moment I'm in.
I promise to listen, take it all in.
I promise to do everything in my power.
I promise to do this, so we can grow wiser.

//Touch the fire

My Heart is Not for Sale

My heart is not for sale,
You cannot buy it, dear.
There's nothing you can pay,
That will make me hand-it-over here.

My heart is not for sale,
It's priceless, everlasting.
It's preciousness eternal,
It's magic spell casting.

My heart is not for sale,
It's value irreplaceable.
A portal of great worth,
It's treasure unmistakable.

My heart is not for sale,
It can only be for giving.
And when it's open, offering,
It Shares its wisdom, singing.

My heart is something special,
It must be cherished to receive.
And when it's given, trusting,
It'll show you how to believe.

//In Honor of a Sacred Heart

I Am

I recently travelled
To the back of my heart…
The place where
The light doesn't shine.
And what I discovered
Are all the parts,
I wish that weren't mine…

In meeting this,
I also found
A hidden depth of wholeness,
And in that place
A whole new me,
A me, that didn't know this:

I Am light,
And I Am shadow…
I Am deep,
And I Am narrow.

I Am complex,
And I'm clear…
I Am wild,
And I Am dear.

I Am healing,
And I'm hurting…
I Am whole,
And I Am learning.

I Am searching,
And I roam…
I Am here,
And I Am home.

I Am wise,
And I Am ignorant…
I Am future, past,
And currant.

I Am grounded,
I Am earth…
I Am the stars,
And I Give birth.

I Am strong,
And I Am weak…
I Stay silent,
And I speak.

I Am this,
And I Am that…
I reject,
And I attract.

I Am big,
And I Am small…
I Am One,
And I Am all.

I Share most
Where I feel safest.
And when I share,
I feel the greatest.

// Polarity Play

Radical self-acceptance says:
"I am what I say I am."

Radical self-responsibility says:
"I am what you say I am."

Go back in…
When there is tension, tears, and trauma.

Go back in…
When there is chaos, confusion, compression.

Go back in…
When it's hard, hopeless, and hurtful.

Go back in…
When there is fear, friction, and fatigue.

Go back in…
And find freedom.

Shame Reframe

Shame comes to show me,
Where I've lost respect.
Where my methods are lacking,
The quality, "I" expect.

It's a pivot in service,
Where I'm learning to grow.
Where I want to do better,
My heart saying, "I know."

It's experience sharing,
The wisdom I hold.
It's a beautiful gift,
And it's time to unfold.

A new stage of development,
A higher path to explore.
"I Am ready" it says,
"Ready for more. "

It's time now to listen,
It's time to step up.
It's time to surrender,
To shift what's been stuck.

//Expanding

Shades of the sky

When the day is bright,
And it's dark at night.
Who is wrong?
And who is right?

Surly, neither?
Why the fight?
Because I Am day?
And you are night?

We feel the contrast,
Know our roles.
To create in daylight,
And rest at night.

So, settle down,
Don't start a war.
Both are needed.
Stop keeping score.

Evolve to peace.
And know your place,
If you're taking turns
No need to race.

No need for tension
In separation,
We're just on other ends,
Of an endless spectrum.

We'll meet again…
And weeks pass by,
Formless knowing
Shades of the sky.

//Beyond Duality

Two Parts of One

Naturally our different decisions,
Take us off in different directions…
As we learn different lessons,
Along the way.

And may we agree,
To cross paths in peace…
As we are bound.
To meet each other again.

And when the journey overlaps
And our vision closes gaps,
May we remember…
We were always One
At the start.

It was just an illusion,
A function of confusion…
That we were ever really,
One of two parts.

// Peace in Conflicting Needs

Soul's Direction

At edges of awareness,
Are the limits of my love.
The places I must stop,
Take time to look above.

In these moments finding stillness,
To listen to my heart.
It's where I start to grow the most,
Feeling deeply is my art.

At the edges of awareness,
I must zoom out to see connection.
Bringing unity into focus,
To remember my soul's direction.

//Unity Consciousness

I've died 1000 deaths.
Just to meet you here,
I have died 1000 deaths.
Only now, I can see clear.

I have died 1000 deaths.
There's still more to discover,
I have died 1000 deaths.
What's 1000 more, I wonder?

I have died 1000 deaths.
I keep finding deeper love,
I have died 1000 deaths.
Each time I rise above.

I have died 1000 deaths.
I'll die again, just to get closer,
I will die 1000 deaths…
Each time a different answer.

What is suppressed,
Will express,
Through the nearest open channel.

Come Closer

I pushed through, I was tired…
Then couldn't.
My heart gave no more,
It wouldn't.
This cycle must stop,
I Am empty.
Nothing left to give,
I Am ready…

Change comes at the end,
When it's over.
The surrender will follow,
       -     Roller coaster.
This is not what I want,
       -     Come closer.
All I need now is peace,
       -     Closure.

"Hold on, don't give up,
Keep trying.
There is beauty to follow,
Start flying.
You can't use your legs,
When you're falling.
It's time to start flapping,
Not walking.

Do you see how you change,
When you need to?
If you just open up
And conceded to.
Evolution is big,
It transforms us.
There are forces,
We must learn to trust.

It's scary at first,
To surrender.
I will stand in your strength,
In your splendor.
We'll do it together,
Connection.
I may need some help,
Some direction.

// Tears for Truth

When I Am Ready

I Release when I Am ready.

When there is no remorse…
When there is no resentment…
When there is no regret.

I Release when I Am ready.

When there is recognition…
When there is reason…
When there is resolve.

I Release when I Am ready,

Into the refuge
Which was always here…
Waiting for me to remember.

// Letting Go

To grow we must hold onto things.
To grow we must release things.

When we can clearly discern the difference, we release what no longer serves our greatest creations.

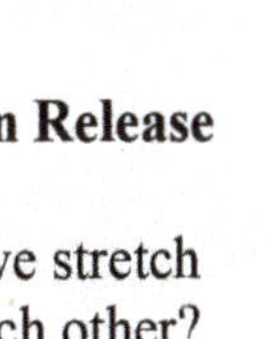

In Release

Can we stretch
To meet each other?
Can we bridge
The gap?

Can we rise
To see the view?
Can we draw
The map?

Can we share Responsibility?
Can we both agree
It's ours?

Can we recognise
Our Oneness?
Can we realise
Our powers?

Can we just stop
Asking questions?
And settle into peace…
Can we choose
To see the beauty,
And surrender
In release.

//Found In Peace

Who knows what will happen?
The next step that I take…
I am clear on direction.
What will it create?

I want to explore there,
Walk lightly with care…
I don't know what will happen,
What will I find there?

Who will I meet?
Why did they stay?
What world did they leave?
And are they soon on their way?

You don't have to be lost,
To explore the unknown.
You can know who you are,
And have space yet to grow.

There's a price to be paid.
When you walk out the door.
There's so much to discover,
Magic and more…

This feels risky,
This feels right…
This feels exciting,
Turn up the light!

This feels meaningful,
This feels new…
This feels fulfilling,
Can it be True?

These Are the Ones

Who are the Ones who inspire your heart?

The Ones who've felt the deepest.
These are the Ones who make you full…
The Ones who've found the sweetness.

Who are the Ones standing brave and tall?

The Ones who've come the farthest.
These are the Ones who show the way…
The Ones who've grown the largest.

Who are the Ones who walk in strength?

The Ones who walk with grace.
These are the Ones to start the prayer…
The Ones who hold the space.

Who are the Ones to surrender fully?

The Ones who trust the most.
These are the Ones who make it clear…
The Ones who weave with hope.

Who are the Ones who shine the light?

The Ones who've met the darkness.
These are the Ones who guide us home…
The Ones who've worked the hardest.

Who are the Ones who speak the truth?

The Ones who've seen potential.
These are the Ones who travel distance…
The Ones who bridge the exponential.

Who are the Ones who know what to ask?

The Ones who've learned to listen.
These are the Ones who value silence…
The Ones who hold the vision.
Who are the Ones who meet the need?

The Ones who've crossed the line.
These are the Ones who've learnt through pain…
The Ones who bow to the divine.

//Ancient Ones

To No End...

To explore everything
To know, Who Am I?

To trust the process
To see I Am evolving.

To forgive myself
To accept I Am learning.

To feel everything I can
To embody I Am human.

To eat only what I need
To honor I Am sacred.

To question everything
To understand I Am One.

To serve myself
To know I Am enough.

To connect with nature
To remember I Am whole.

To reach my potential
To realise I Am limitless.

To change fearlessly
To evolve for the greater good.

To run fearlessly toward the unknown
To discover All that is sacred.

To no end…
To remember I Am timeless.

//Limitless

Discover You

How warmly can I greet you
When the journey circles back?
How sweetly did I say goodbye
When I took the inside track?

How often did I say, "I miss you."?
Not enough…
I don't know why.
I felt alive with the changes,
That I can't deny.

When we meet again, I trust
There will be so much more to share…
The space between us only
Helps to make us more aware.

We can't always be united,
To accept this brings great peace,
I feel this with a gentle sigh
As tension is released…

I see, no gap is too big to bridge,
If both are willing to adjust.
And no connection is too close to cut
For those who need to grow in trust.

It can be hard to know ourselves at times,
We walk that path alone.
And yet when I'm listening carefully,
I hear the song of the unknown.

We can only give what is within us,
I'm discovering great treasure…
To share them once I've found them,
Brings me the greatest pleasure.

We were always serving one another,
This much I know is true.
We just needed different things at times,
I hope that you discovered…

YOU.

//In Separation

You & Me

I did it for you,
There's a cost to me.
I did it for you,
Now I see…

I did it for you,
What an honor,
I did it for you
Now you seem warmer.

I did it for me.
There's a cost to you.
I did it for me,
And growth pushed through.

I did it for me.
And I've seen you flourish,
I did it for me,
Now we're both nourished.

//All Sides

It's time for me to walk my path,
And continue on my way.
New worlds of wonder are a calling,
"Keep walking", wise ones say.

I wish you well, and blessings.
As you continue to explore.
For me, now, though, it is time to go,
And offer service somewhere more.

Farewell beloveds - thank you!
There have been so many memories made.
I've closed a loop in wholeness,
I'm no longer afraid.

There was beauty here,
And now there's not…
A space revealed
An open spot.

You've had your turn…
Now settle down.
It's time for new seeds
Left to ground.

Teacher Tay Turns 5

This little mirror I call Tay,
Your shining light shows me the way.

In rainbow dreams, you're pure of heart…
With all the ways you love to craft.

You lead me up a path of magic,
It's inside you, totally organic.

It may take time for me to see,
All the ways you're guiding me…

Deep down inside I know it's true,
The reason I know love,
Is you.

// In Spirit

Oh Tay…

Oh Tay…
What can I say?
Your shining light
Brightens up my day.

Oh Tay…
Where do you get it?
This endless affection
Never misses.

Oh Tay…
You're a blessing.
A true inspiration
I'm confessing.

Oh Tay…
Never stop.
Heart open
Your love's on top.

//The Way of Tay

To Troy, In Love.

My first-born son,
You made me "Mom".
Your deep blue love
So pure and calm.

Every day with you
Is love.
You anchor light
From up above.

To Troy, in Love,
I hope you know,
Because of you,
I always grow.

I'll always love you
This is true,
Because you are me
And I am you.

//Deep Blue Boy

This is how we Stand

The path isn't always easy –
Truth tells me the journey is always worth it.

We aren't always in the same place –
Space shows me we're always going in the same direction.

We can't always see the same picture –
Time shows me we always hold the same vision.

And All of it for the Blessing of our Integrated Love.

To those who walk ahead of us, we bow.
With those who walk besides us, we smile.
For those who walk behind us, we honor.

// In Marriage

These Beautiful Humans

Teach me everyday,
Show me a brighter way.

Shower us in love,
Connected up above.

Inspire me to see,
Beauty inside me.

Honored to be "Mom",
Light me up with magic charms.

Grateful they've come here,
I hope to always have them near.

I was lucky to be open,
To receive this vision token.

One day they'll learn to fly,
By then I'll be the sky…

// In Motherhood

A tribute to all those who come next and their power in innocence.
Inspired by my children who see the world in new ways for all beings.

Come Back for Birthdays

Come back for birthdays
And holiday feasts,
Come back for gatherings
Where we can meet…

As our wings and the wind
Take us off in all ways
Come back for moments…
Grandmother says.

Let's celebrate life
And how far we have come,
Let's all get together…
Together as One.

//Together as One

When examining boundaries,
My limits hold firm.
The pieces of me
Not yet willing to learn.

These are the spaces,
I Am
Integrating,
The truth of duality
My heart
Liberating.

Some lessons are learned,
No need to revisit.
So my role changes now,
In service, I pivot.

There's a process to follow,
No shame in the journey.
"It's all by design…
It's all Love",
I hear faintly.

At times like these
It can be hard to find.
The right things
To say…

So, in the space
Now opened up
I hope,
You find your way…

With every loss
There's change to come.
Healing
If you let it…

There's only love.
Anchor in,
The heart
Will always know it.

The Dreams in Me

I hold dreams in me,
They have a cost.

I hold dreams in me,
They won't get lost.

When I question them,
They grow stronger.

They're not only mine…
They've waited longer.

I hold dreams in me,
Sometimes I judge them.

I hold dreams in me,
Who do they belong to?

When I listen closely,
I know they're ours…

So, I'll follow dreams,
I trust their powers.

And when they're realised…
Perhaps I'll see,
There was no difference
Between Me and We.

//In Dreams

Magic in Moments

And then finally…
A dream comes true!
You have no idea
How I've waited for you!

As joy begins
To flood my heart
A lightness returns…
I am back at a start.

A brand new chapter
A new potential
Love opened a door…
Quintessential.

A smile begins
To flood my face,
It's been so long…
This feels so strange!

How did I doubt you?
The path, the way…
-   *"You've been here before"*
You seem to Say.

The recognition of
-Up and Down-
This too shall pass
I Think with a frown…

But not today!
Today I'm here!
So, I'll cherish Now,
I'll hold it Dear.

Yes, this will change
And that's okay…
What makes it magic
Is that it's here today.

//Realisation

Jewels from the Journey

I found humility in arrogance,
And pleasure in the pain.
I found kindness in the wounding,
And the will to start again.

I found trust in the anxiety,
And faith in the unknown.
I found clarity in confusion,
Through all of it…
I've grown.

All I had to do was open,
And hold it in my heart.
All I had to do was trust it,
And allow the change to start.

Emotions came to teach me,
And now they're my heart's tools.
To show me back to Oneness,
And share the journey's jewels.

//Self Discovery

Capacity of Togetherness

To all the people,
Who I made wrong.
I'm sorry for my ignorance.

For all the times
I made you right,
I'm sorry for my ignorance.

For all the ways
I found division,
I'm sorry for my ignorance.

The dissolving illusion of wrong & right
Has me questioning my direction.
But when I go inwards, and choose my heart,
I Am home and in connection.

What do I need?
Can I surrender?
And meet you in Awareness…
The place that knows,
That where love grows,
In capacity of togetherness.

Some dreams are quick to realise,
Some dreams take time to find.
Some dreams want to be nurtured,
Some dreams aren't even mine.

Some dreams feel like they take forever,
Do dreams always come true?
Some dreams want me to hold them,
The next generation, due.

Some dreams are living presence,
Some dreams were gifts to me.
Some dreams are my experience,
Now I'll be planting seeds.

How do you leave when it's time to go?
Do you throw up your hands and yell out "NO!"

How do you leave when you've grown up?
Do you wave goodbye, and then get stuck?

How do you leave when times have changed?
Do you fade in the distance, become estranged?

How do you leave once you've been of service?
Do you bow in thanks and leave the circus?

How do you leave when life has ended?
Do you close your eyes, all as intended.

As endings begin,
I feel my heart,
The expansion of change
The spark of a start.

A new beginning
Is on its way
We're all in love
"Together"
I pray.

Love is Triumphant

The things that used to make me happy…
They don't anymore.
Like the value's disappeared,
Nothing
Left
To
Explore.

It's from this place,
I must go deeper.
No more fear,
Or threat of judgement.
A new world is revealing
Where love becomes triumphant.

//Love Leads the Way

Rainbow Wonders

There was madness,
And magic.
A safe space,
And mind tricks.

In the chaos
And confusion
A release
Of the illusion…

As I forget and remember.
What I learn is, Love's forever.
There is only love, It's always near,
Come meet your heart, It's right in here.

Just settle down,
In stillness.
Bring peace.
And anchor wellness.

What's real,
Is all the colors.,
Of the rainbow,
And its wonders.

//There is Only Love

Back home to Love

The bias of belonging
The illusion of belief,
The denial of righteous knowing
Has me slipping into grief…

The ignorance of separateness,
The lack of deep connection.
The need to council "others"
The joy of imperfection.

Distortions of the journey,
Confusion on the path.
An infinite experience
Back home to love at last.

All By Design

In the muck of despair,
In the grips of fear…
In the throes of anxiety,
What do I need to hear?

There seems to be endless disfunction,
Undeniable grief.
What does this want to teach me?
When is there relief?

If I'm present with all of it.
Let all of it in…
Won't I become darkness?
Won't I become sin?

I Am whole in my being,
There is nothing not mine.
It all comes to show me,
The expanse of divine.

What role can I play here?
How do I stand tall?
Who can I lead?
We all take a fall…

And so, getting back up,
I remember my way.
I am here for the loving,
When I'm quiet, they say:

"You're held my beloved,
Trust the process, in time.
You'll bloom through the pressure,
It's all by design."

//Power In Pressure

New Beginnings

In the depths of desperation,
Is a need that wants to know…
This too shall pass, beloved,
Surrender, let it flow.

All is valid, All is necessary.
Allow this moment to exist.
It's all within you – blooming.
Held in love, it can't persist.

In the stillness of this moment,
Is a magic which transforms…
All experiences to purpose
Evolution must perform.

In the light of realization,
Comes a peace that soothes the heart.
In the presence of acceptance,
New beginnings found to start.

//Acceptance of this Now Moment

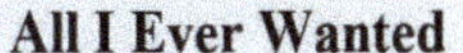

All I Ever Wanted

Not getting what I wanted,
I found a gift I never got.
In the gap of expectation,
I discovered a whole lot.

New dimensions were revealed to me,
In the space between my dreams.
In the waiting room of wanting,
A bigger vision starts to gleam.

There's so much to imagined,
Even more to be explored.
Being open to the flow of life –
All I ever wanted and more…

//Limitless

HOME

I call myself Home

I call myself home,
To my heart.
This is my center,
It's where I start.

I trust the journey,
As it unfolds…
I know the way,
It's mine to mold.

And when I sit here peacefully,
The stillness comes,
It's inside me.

And with this knowing,
I surrender,
It's in the mystery
That I wander.

// It feels good to give your heart away. Give your heart away where it feels good.

Words & worlds discovered with my friend Candice Goldring through authentic relating.

We Are One

If love is presence and connection,
And truth is space and time,
I trust we'll come together,
In the place where we are One.

If I can let love flow,
And you can anchor me,
I know we'll meet, together,
Beneath the old oak tree.

We are one,
United.
We are One,
At last.
We are One,
Together.
We are One
Everything surpassed.

In my heart I'm whole now,
As we close the gap at last.
It felt, to me, like forever.
Since we cleared the past.

We are one,
United.
We are One,
At last.
We are One,
Together.
We are One
Everything surpassed.

// Weaving Unity

God *[verb]*

The universal process of the unknown discovering itself.

Peace is a place in our hearts that is earned not only by accepting, respecting and allowing the past to have happened
but through embracing, caring and honoring the blessings we have been given,
regardless how they have come to us.

Through this, forgiveness is no longer necessary and only gratitude remains.
It is from this place we anchor love in the now and create brighter futures for those who come next.

The Mountains Called

The mountains called,
So here I Am.
The mountains called,
They have a plan.

To see their beauty,
Is the cure.
Breathe in their presence,
Strong and pure.

The sunrise gently
Warms my face.
Above the clouds,
In God's grace.

The grasses sweep,
My path is clear.
The streams wash clean,
Now I can hear.

The wind breathes strong,
A Storm passes through.
When it is done,
All anew.

Light filters down,
As seeds are sown.
Back down the summit,
Slowly home…

// Coming Home

Mamma Africa

Have you ever been somewhere
With space for it all?

The home of humanity
She'll send out a call.

With all of her beauty
And a wildness of heart,

There's a magic of home
It's where we all start.

Dear Mamma Africa
This is where I belong.

I Am yours to create
I will sing out your song.

Your wisdom abounds
It's too big to see…

The place that I found
The land of opportunity.

// Roots

Two things can be true at once,
And I know what my heart needs.
Embracing conflict opens up
A space that holons seed.

Leaders speak their truth.
It is here we make our home.
Prophets say "Everyone is truth",
As we explore the great unknown.

It was here all along,
I just couldn't see it.
It was here all along,
I couldn't believe it.

This beauty,
This peace,
This undeniable heaven.
It was here all along,
I just couldn't see it.

What Remains

Do you see what I see?
I don't think that you do…
Our experiences, perspectives
Set the point of view.

Do you feel what I feel?
I know that you do…
My emotions, sensations
Feel the same as you.

Do we dream the same dream?
Perhaps at times…
Our desires, intentions
Knit together in rhymes.

Will you visit me here?
We all walk our own path…
Our choices, directions
Take us off in one half.

Step into my world…
And I'll do the same.
Our love and connection,
Will always remain.

//Heart Space

The Work of Light

The subtle art of surrender,
Doesn't mean
I must consent.
It's not that I allow the force,
To take away my strength.

Surrender's not
An everlasting "Yes",
I allow and see what is.
I choose to work.
Be more aware.
And the healing
That this gives.

Darkness belongs to all of us,
It's mine,
It's ours,
I'd say…

The light is here
To guide me,
I open up and Pray:

*May the eternal truth
Of One guide me,
May the path be
Clear and bright.
May pure source
Nourish what I need,
May I do
The work of Light.*

//Prayers for Peace

Commitment is one of those hard-earned virtues…
It can only be tested in time.
It's through all of the good times,
and hard times too,
We go deeper into the divine.

There are times we will dance,
There are times we will cry,
There are times when we'll want it to end.
And on the other side of that, my dear,
Is a time where love transcends.

As above,
So below.
From the roots
Branches grow.

As is deep,
Is my love.
So, the view
From above.

As I dive
Through compassion
I discover,
My hearts passion.

One by one
We all follow.
"Only Love"
My new motto.

Safe is your Love

So safe is your love,
That
I Am
Free.
So safe is your love,
That
I Am
Me.

The anchor of trust,
Undeniable strength.
Because you are you,
My limits, no end.

So safe is your love.
That
I Am
Whole.
So Safe is your love,
I
Express
My
Soul.

//Jiva
These are the gifts from my grandmother, Dawn.

Touching the Divine

I may be going crazy,
I see mirrors everywhere…
No One is separate, in this place,
Love is ours to share.

Touching the divine,
There's so much more to give.
No matter where I'm called to serve
I trust this life I live.

It might feel tense, unsettling.
There may be conflict too,
When arriving back to love at last,
I remember,
I Am You.

Share all of what is needed,
Let my heart lead on the way.
"You can't go wrong when anchored,
And connected", prophet's say.

Take my journey with you,
As we walk the path of light.
As an offering through me
We do the work of God.

Take my journey with you,
through the beauty of reality.
Each magical creation,
A reflection of vitality.

Take my journey with you,
It belongs to all of us.
As we weave it into prayers,
Embodied consciousness.

There's a knowing in my heart,
It's solid and unshakable.
A feeling so enlightening
No doubt,
Is unmistakable.

As light pours in,
Transforming.
"Why me?"
No need for answers…

"Be still and know."
It tells me.
I Am quiet, gently smiling.

I bow to the divine,
The power ever humbling.
I'm ready to make offerings,
Life force replenished
Summoning.

I receive the blessing,
Thankful.
A promise to the light…
I'll do your work ongoing,
I know the way,
All
Right.

Love is the Flare

The ground that illuminates,
With the glow of your love.
Where seeds can be planted,
And warmed from above.

This magic ability
To be in both worlds,
One of anchoring darkness
And shining light that unfurls.

This is your beauty,
Of wholeness with care.
Bringing deep understanding,

That love is the flare.

//Illumination

Because of You

Because of you,
I'm better than before…
Because of you,
I've grown.

Because of you,
I'm bigger than I was.
Because of you,
I know.

Because of you,
I trust myself.
Because of You,
The seeds are sewn.

Because of you,
I rest in peace.
Because of you,
I'm home.

//Home In Love

I hold a Vision

I hold a vision of a world that understands,
Corruption, control, and dominance.
A world that becomes honest, collaborative, and supportive of all beings.

I hold a vision of a world that allows,
Pollution, waste, and decay.
A world becoming pure, sustainable, and transformational.

I hold a vision of a world with space,
For suffering, scarcity & polarity.
A world that is healed, abundant and united.

I hold a vision of a world that recognizes,
Assumptions, powerlessness, and limitations.
A world that is creative, empowered and transcending.

I hold a vision of a world that surrenders,
To anger, hatred and fear.
I hold a vision of a world that is,
Free to choose its creation.

A world that chooses love.

When I look within…
You are me,
We are one.

// In Heaven

Way Shower

As I sit here in stillness,
In silence,
I open my heart,
To your guidance…

I trust my
Intentions in service,
I wish to deliver,
Your purpose.

Show me what to do,
And I'll listen.
In honor of you,
The path glistens.

Wherever there's beauty
I'll follow.
Together we create,
Our tomorrow.

//Glimmers

You'll know when I greet you,
In person, by name.
Divine recognition,
We're One and the same.

You'll know when our eyes meet,
Connection in focus.
Behind the illusion,
Undeniable closeness.

You'll know as I listen,
Together, be proud.
No hiding from joy,
Loving out loud.

In degrees of separation
Can we find it in our hearts,
The courage to be kind.
Oneness pieces of the parts.

It takes strength to remain open,
To bear witness in neutrality.
Trust the value of diversity
And the wisdom to find clarity.

Choices take us in directions,
All is valid, all is necessary.
Can I find a deeper love?
How can I serve humanity?

Beyond the Borders of Our Bloodline

Beyond the borders of our bloodline…
Is a journey you must travel.
Beyond the borders of our bloodline…
Is an adventure, waiting to unravel.

Beyond the borders of our bloodline…
Is a horizon you can't see.
Beyond the borders of our bloodline…
Is a magic mystery.

Beyond the borders of our bloodline…
Awaits the deepest sense of truth.
Beyond the borders of our bloodline…
The fountain of everlasting youth.

Beyond the borders of our bloodline…
Is a purpose come to call.
Beyond the borders of our bloodline…
Is to serve the One and All.

// Beyond Bloodline

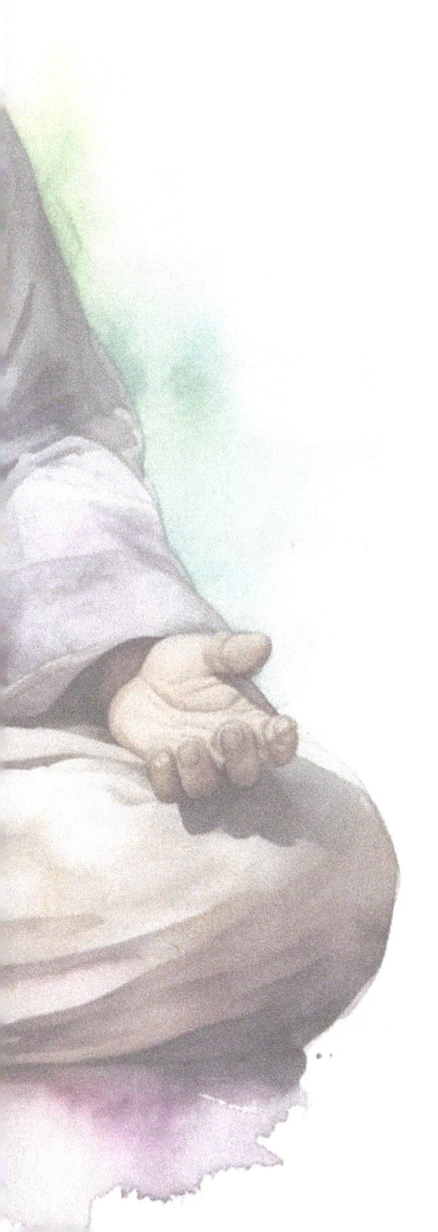

Resting in Enough

Resting in enough,
There is nothing more I need.
Resting in enough,
There is nothing left to seed.

Resting in enough,
I have Everything to give.
Resting in enough,
All I want is to live.

Resting in enough,
I Am whole and I am peaceful.
Resting in enough,
I Am full and I am grateful.

Resting in enough,
I take nothing more for granted.
Resting in enough,
I have all I ever wanted.

//In Gratitude

The Wheel of Oneness

The wheel of Oneness
Has no "one-way",
The wheel of Oneness
Here to
Stay.

It shows us how
We're all connected,
Reminds us how
The divine
Directs us.

Full spectrum spans
Across its surface,
All experiences
Have a
Purpose.

The rainbow light,
Comes shining through,
With all the colors,
Blending
You.

As you embody
All that Is,
The wheel of Oneness
Only
Gives.

// In One

We cannot go alone.
All come.
We all arrive together.
As we are all One.

END

(Not really...Not ever.)

Cloud of Love.

With this cloud of Love I Ask,
For all the Angels give this Task...

Keep my children safe Tonight,
Shower them in Loving Light.

Keep them safe for All of Time.
With a Mother's Love Divine.

Safe In Love.
Safe In Love,
Safe In Love
For All of Time.

*// **Sweet Dreams***

I Clear, I Cleanse,
I Open Up...

I Breathe, I Balance,
I Fill My Cup.

I Call in Self, I Call in Spirit,
I wish to be of Service in it.

*//**Prayers of Service***